THE SOUND OF BELLS

Doubleday Books by Eric Sloane

The Sound of Bells
ABC Book of Early Americana:
  A Sketchbook of Antiquities and American Firsts

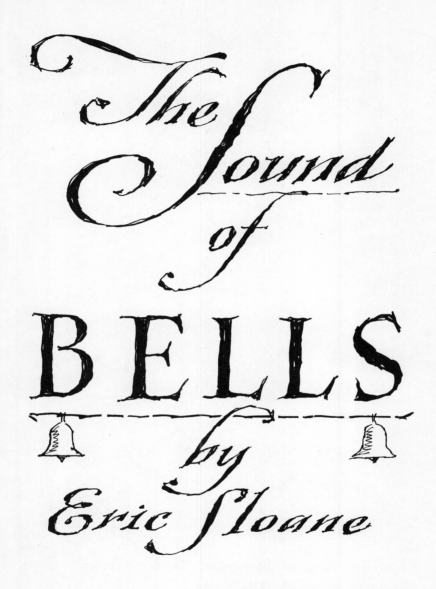

The Sound of BELLS

by Eric Sloane

DOUBLEDAY & COMPANY, INC., GARDEN CITY, NEW YORK

Library of Congress Catalog Card Number 66–12672
Copyright © 1966 by Eric Sloane
All Rights Reserved
Printed in the United States of America

Author's Note

If it were not for Independence Day, this book would not have been written, for the subject of bells does not immediately seem of much importance in the history of America. Yet a few years ago when I noticed the frequent mention of Independence Day bells in early diaries and eighteenth-century account books, I began to wonder. Back in 1957 when I wrote *The Seasons of America Past*, I first realized that bells had a special place in Americana.

"When Chinese firecrackers entered the scene," I wrote, "Independence Day bell-ringing vanished. But the thought of church bells and farm bells and school bells and fire bells all clanging through the countryside seems best to catch the spirit of that first great American day. It would be fitting, it seems, to revive the bells of Independence Day."

A few years later when my neighbor Eric Hatch joined with me to make my dream come true, President Kennedy made a proclamation, a resolution was passed in the U. S. Congress, and state proclamations were made urging that Independence Day be celebrated "this year and on every year following by the ringing of bells." Already there are small children who think this was always an uninterrupted custom; children who have never shot off a firecracker but who now look forward to ringing bells on July Fourth.

Now after more than four years of working on the Independence Day bell project, it seems that the revival has taken hold. The "bell room" where my wife, along with Eric Hatch and his wife, had kept office handling the ton or so of mail that poured in, has now become a bedroom again. And the next job seems to be that of getting bells to American children; for the bells can't be rung unless there are bells to be had.

So there you are with an explanation for this book, *The Sound of Bells.* I hope that it might not only enrich the lore of Americana, but also, and perhaps more important, that it might enrich the lives of many young Americans.

Eric Sloane
Weather Hill
Warren, Connecticut

THE SOUND OF BELLS

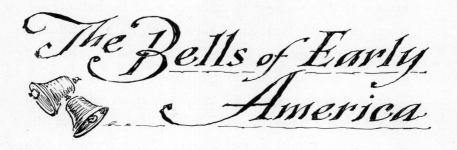

The Bells of Early America

The sounds of America were once good to hear. Not the unnerving noises of automobiles and vacuum cleaners and factory whistles and airplanes and sirens and the clatter of garbage pails and the screech of brakes and horns. Instead there was a comforting serenity.

In the winter there were the slithery squeals of sled runners and the soft clip-clop of horses' hoofs in the snow. There were also sleigh bells which made almost continuous winter music. In the summer the scissors grinder and rag picker and street vendor went from street to street calling out, and they were always ringing a handbell.

At night the stillness was often broken by the distant wail of the old-time steam locomotive; this could be sad or joyous or lonesome or adventurous, according to your own mood. But it was always music, never just noise. When the train whistle ceased, you could still hear the locomotive's bell which was big and clangorous, and it seemed to continue as if by habit, even when the train had come to a halt. As the drawing shows, the locomotive bell had a heavy counterbalance which helped keep it swinging back and forth.

As you approached any early American village, you would always hear the soft thump and splash of the old-time grist mill water wheels. What sounded like distant thunder usually turned out to be the hollow roar of some horse and wagon going through the wooden tunnel of a covered bridge. Even in the heart of town, if you listened carefully, you might hear the sounds of outlying farms, of cows and chickens and the constant tinkle of cow bells.

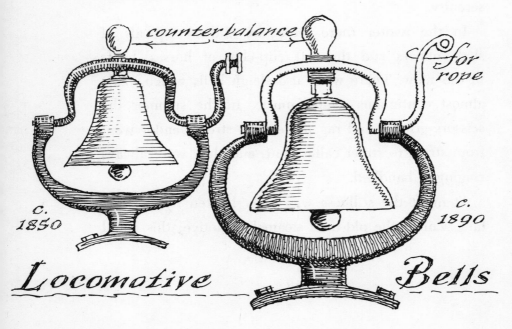

counterbalance

for rope

c. 1850

c. 1890

Locomotive *Bells*

At the end of day, when the big squat iron farm dinner bells began to sound, cows took it as a signal to wander in the direction of their barns, and all the sounds of the countryside began to quiet. But most commanding and carrying and respected was the voice of the great town bell and church bell. In their

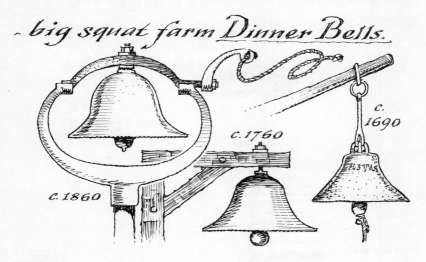

big squat farm Dinner Bells.

C. 1690

C. 1760

C. 1860

belfries, whenever their mouths opened to the countryside and the thunderous tones of bell sound floated over the surrounding hills, all the people listened.

At first, when meeting houses served both as town hall and place of worship, the building was simple, either square or round and without any belfry or steeple on top. A bell was either hung from a nearby tree or from a "bell pole," high enough to cast the sound of the bell over the rooftops and on to distant

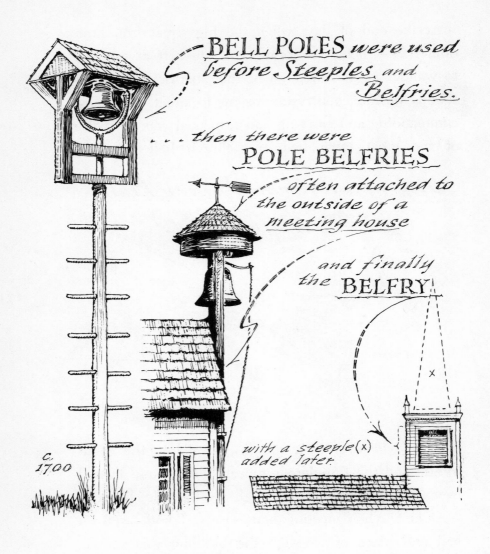

BELL POLES *were used before Steeples and Belfries.*

...then there were POLE BELFRIES *often attached to the outside of a meeting house*

and finally the BELFRY

with a steeple(x) added later.

c. 1700

farms. Later, there was a double poled bell, hanging with the bell swinging between the two poles, and this contraption was fastened directly to the building. Finally, of course, the bell was housed in a belfry

16

as an actual part of the building and during later years a steeple was sometimes added on top of the belfry.

At first, these great bells did not call out the hour as they do nowadays, but they did sound three special hours of the day. At six in the morning there was a signal to remind everyone that day was already in progress and that all was well. It was time to begin work. At twelve there was a noon bell, the signal for lunching and that period known to the early farmer as "nooning" or resting. At nine in the evening there was a signal for retiring known as curfew. In the earliest days of America when roofs were thatched with grass, this bell asked that all people bank or cover their fires so that they might not flare up during the night. So this bell was called by its French name, *couvre feu* or the "cover-fire bell," and then became the English "curfew bell." The couvre-feu custom of colonial days was also protection against marauding Indians; how strange that our modern word curfew harks back to so primitive a custom.

Just as different cities have different customs, many early villages had their own special bell signals. Those near the sea might tell of rising tides or the arrivals of fishing fleets. Some curfew bells were followed by sharp strokes to indicate the date of the month to aid those making diary entries before retiring for the night. In case of fires, some town bells had a code that told in what area of the countryside the fire was. It was all like a Morse code and it was quite necessary, for there were no other means of communication.

The church bell (never the town bell) tolled death knells, either during the funeral or after the morning town bell had finished. Death knells were "two times three" for a woman and "three times three" for a man. These funeral sounds were all made by hand, with a soft wooden mallet, sometimes known as a "dead striker," and the sound was solemn and muffled. In some places, the deceased's age was tolled (told) by striking that exact number, one strike every minute. Called a "minute bell," this would take an hour and a half for a ninety-one-year-old person.

At Christmas Eve there was a midnight "Devil's Knell" rung for Satan who was said to have "died when Christ was born." Christmas Day ringing in New England began at seven in the morning and ended at four in the afternoon, but the whole day was known as an American Day of Bells.

Although the word *toll* originally meant to "tell," and *knell* indicated sadness, the word knell ceased

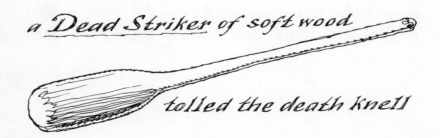

a *Dead Striker* of soft wood

tolled the death knell

to be used when funerals were "tolled." Here is an early rhyme which tells something of bell language. Copied from a sampler, it helped children to learn the messages that bells had to tell:

When we lament a departed soul, WE TOLL.
When joy and mirth are on the wing, WE SING.
To call the fold to church in time, WE CHIME.
When threatened harm, WE ALARM.

An alarm was given by a continuous ringing or a steady tattoo (with iron rods) or by grasping the clapper of a handbell and striking it continuously in a quick manner. Anyone hearing such an alarm would consider it a call for immediate help.

With all these bell messages, one might imagine the various codes difficult to learn, and the days all but shattered by the sounds. Yet it was taken for granted, for without bells it would be like our present day without telephones or radio. People enjoyed their town and church bells and they often spoke proudly about "how far their bells could be heard" or about "their rare or fine tone." Some could even foretell the weather by the sound of a distant bell, for when the air pressure lowers as it does before a rain, a bell

Striking a bell directly and continuously with its own clapper was an old "S.O.S." signal

does change its tone, sounding as if it were in a long hollow corridor. Under ideal circumstances, the average limit of bell sound is nine miles, but there is one record during a fire alarm, where a bell (in Kennebunk, Maine) was heard plainly eleven miles away (in Alfred, Maine). Generally speaking, a big bell's sound carries better than a rifle shot.

The old-time pranksters had many opportunities with their town and church bells. A favorite April Fool trick was to wrap cloth around the church bell's clapper so that little or no sound came from its striking. Another was to tie a string to the clapper and hiding at a safe distance, to start pulling away at midnight and rouse the whole village.

The Sabbath Day used to be strictly observed, but it was not held during the day of Sunday as it is today; it began at sundown on Saturday and ended at sunset on Sunday. Both the starting and ending times of the Sabbath were rung by the church bell. Knowing how strict and religious the old-timers were, it seems strange that some of the biggest parties were held on Sunday. But, of course, that was after the end of the Sabbath at sundown.

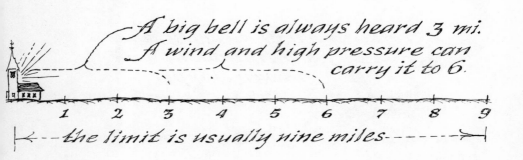

A big bell is always heard 3 mi. A wind and high pressure can carry it to 6.

1 2 3 4 5 6 7 8 9

the limit is usually nine miles

Bells on the Move

People might wonder just why farmers put bells on their animals. We know about cows, of course, and how a belled animal can be located even in a deep forest; yet with a little research we find that cats and dogs and ducks and geese and goats and sheep and even turkeys once had bells of their own design. Some farmers had their cow bells tuned to a certain note so that a lost animal could be identified even at a distance. The lead cow had a huge bell (see drawing) that had a special tone. Geese and turkeys had bells for their own protection as well as identification, for only a century ago the average farm was always troubled with attacks from bears, foxes, wolves, and bobcats.

Most people believe that horse bells were just ornamental and for enjoyment. But bells were a necessary

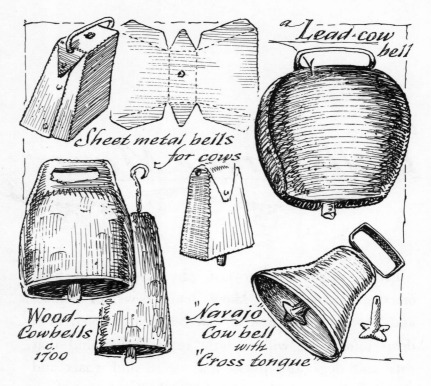

Sheet metal bells for cows

a Lead-cow bell

Wood Cowbells c. 1700

"Navajo" Cow bell with "Cross tongue"

part of winter traffic. Sleighs were fast and silent, while people were usually deafened by earmuffs and mufflers. As there were no sidewalks, people walked in the road, sometimes right in the midst of sleigh traffic, which added to the danger. In a few places in New England, there was even a fine for sleighs that were not properly equipped with bells.

For every wagon he owned, the average farmer of early America had from two to four sleds, for the best roads were those of snow during the winter. During spring and summer, the old dirt roads became

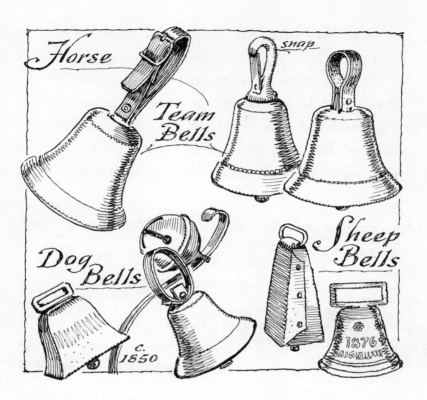

an impassable sea of mud whenever it rained. Wheels just wouldn't turn under a heavy load on the average cross-country road. So all heavy cargo such as logs

or stone was saved till winter and moved easily on runners.

Whereas snow is a present-day nuisance on the streets and highways, at one time in America snow was cherished and saved. It was shoveled from the sides of the road and put into the middle; then it was rolled flat with snow rollers until it was a sheet

Even the insides of Covered Bridges needed Snow in the old days!

of ice-like surface which lasted into the spring of the year. Although most people still think the covered bridges were built to keep out the snow, bridge owners were obliged to shovel snow into their bridges so that the sleds could pass through.

Wagon bells jingled and clanged just from the roughness of the road; they were hung either solidly or were on springs. But sleds moved so evenly on the packed snow that bells had to be put on the harness or trappings of the horses, otherwise they would not jingle. Crotal-type bells could be bought by the pound and sewed to leather straps, and the place where they were made was "Jingletown, U.S.A.," East Hampton, Connecticut. This town was (and still is) the bell capital of America. Yankee peddlers went there to pick up crotals to sell along their routes, buying by the pound and selling them singly. Jingletown's catalogs had as many as five hundred kinds and sizes of bells, but the illustration shows four samples from an old Bevin Brothers list.

Sleigh bells (a misnomer because they were usually used on the horses' harness and not the sleigh) have long been the favorite of the American Indian. Even now you will find that a strap of crotals on each ankle is standard costume for any Indian dancer. When there was an Indian attack on a wagon train, sometimes the greatest prizes were the bells that the teams wore.

Actually the bell was the American Indian's natural musical instrument, for from ancient times they made bell-like rattles from gourds and turtle shells and hollow sticks. The "Indian drum" was really introduced by the white soldiers, and there is no record of the very ancient Indian ever having used drums of any kind.

Indians were supposed to be very superstitious about the sound of bells, and women left at home

The CROTAL was America's sleigh and wagon bell bought by the pound, ... to sew on straps, ... "as many as 500 different kinds."

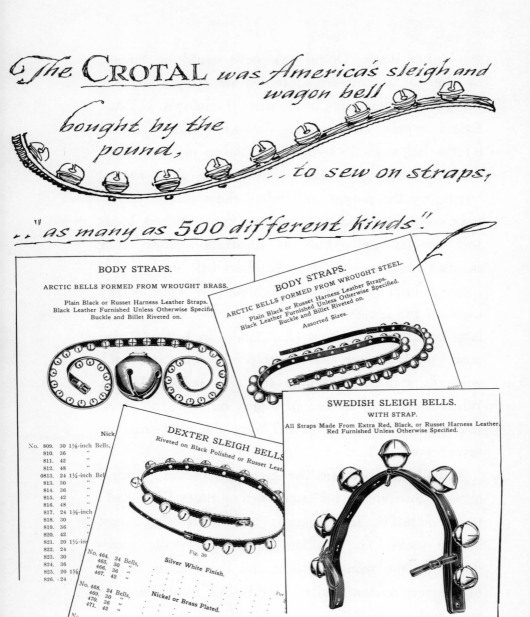

BODY STRAPS.

ARCTIC BELLS FORMED FROM WROUGHT BRASS.

Plain Black or Russet Harness Leather Straps.
Black Leather Furnished Unless Otherwise Specified
Buckle and Billet Riveted on.

BODY STRAPS.

ARCTIC BELLS FORMED FROM WROUGHT STEEL.

Plain Black or Russet Harness Leather Straps.
Black Leather Furnished Unless Otherwise Specified.
Buckle and Billet Riveted on.

Assorted Sizes.

SWEDISH SLEIGH BELLS.

WITH STRAP.

All Straps Made From Extra Red, Black, or Russet Harness Leather.
Red Furnished Unless Otherwise Specified.

DEXTER SLEIGH BELLS.

Riveted on Black Polished or Russet Leath

Fig. 30

Silver White Finish.

Nickel or Brass Plated.

Nick

No.	809.	30	1⅛-inch Bells,
	810.	36	"
	811.	42	"
	812.	48	"
	0813.	24	1¼-inch Bel
	813.	30	"
	814.	36	"
	815.	42	"
	816.	48	"
	817.	24	1⅜-inch
	818.	30	"
	819.	36	"
	820.	42	"
	821.	20	1½-in
	822.	24	
	823.	30	
	824.	36	
	825.	20	1⅝
	826.	24	

No. 464. 24 Bells,
465. 30 "
466. 36 "
467. 42 "

No. 468. 24 Bells,
469. 30 "
470. 36 "
471. 42 "

26

during colonial days, often kept a handbell close by, should there be worry about marauding Indians. Ringing the bell gave "an alarm to neighbors and it frightened the savages, at the same time."

The Indians' habit of putting their ear to the ground to hear approaching horses probably gave rise to their superstitions about the bell, for a big town bell can be heard plainly through the ground when often it cannot be heard because of hills or wind interference. There is one legend in New Hampshire about a village that was covered by a winter's avalanche of snow and rocks which completely buried a small church building. "If you put your ear to the ground," so the story goes, "you can still hear the ghostly church bell ring at midnight." Actually what you would hear is the bell from a nearby town, since the sound may carry remarkably well through the ground.

The large handbell used to call children to school is probably the best-known bell in America, and there are people who collect them as Americana. Actually the first American schoolteachers used tin horns for calling children, and so did the housewives when they called the men in from the fields. It might be presumed that there were once so many bells sounding from so many animals and churches and town halls, that a horn was a more commanding and different signal. Horns and even drums were used for calling people to church during the early 1600's. But by the 1700's the bell had become the national instrument for calling people together.

The largest school bell type was used by the town crier. The town crier of the 1600's and early 1700's rang his bell along with his cry of "All's well" in such a manner to comfort rather than alarm people. For alarm or call for help he kept a "rattler," which was a wooden device that made a very loud noise when twirled around. The author has a rattler from Plymouth, Massachusetts which can be easily heard for two miles. The rattler in later years became the alarm for firemen and policemen and night watchmen.

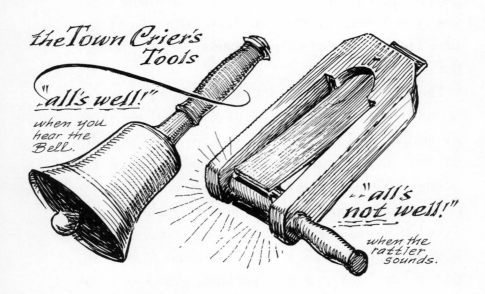

the Town Crier's Tools

"all's well!"
when you
hear the
Bell.

"all's not well!"
when the
rattler
sounds.

The town crier who roamed the streets calling out the hours was not a typically American figure, but there was a town crier in America who called people together in the town square whenever news arrived. Newspapers seldom printed news in the early days; instead they printed *comments* upon news. The reason for this was, that by the time the news was hand set and printed on the old slow presses, it was no longer news. News, of course, had to arrive by a messenger on horseback. It was immediately put up on a town square bulletin board, and a copy was rushed to the printers. The town crier immediately rang his big bell, and people rushed to the bulletin board to read the news while the newspaper was being printed.

The uses of the bell in America were almost numberless, from devices to scare away birds to buoys at sea and wild animal alarms. Just after the Civil War era, when mass production was introduced and factories began to flourish, inventors found even more uses for bells by putting them into all kinds of mechanical devices. Even now, although we might think the bell an outmoded thing, it wakens you in the morning in your alarm clock, it calls you to the telephone, it ends every line on your typewriter, calls you to the door, and does so many things that we are so used to that we seldom notice them.

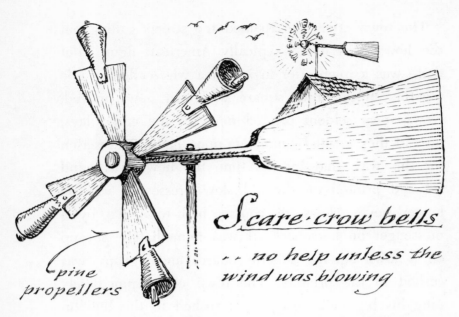

Scare·crow bells

·· no help unless the wind was blowing

pine propellers

The bell is still the standard burglar alarm, but people of colonial times used to use a simple handbell at night, balancing it on the mantel or on a chair and tying a string from it to the doorknob. The Yankee peddler sold a little stand for holding a handbell against the door, so it would tip when the door opened; this was called a bell tilt. Farmers often kept a bell in their kitchen garden with a string to the bedroom; a frequent pull on the string whenever the thought came to mind would keep the raccoons or other destructive animals away.

The spring bell was first used on the early fire-fighting wagons. The rough roadways would jounce the wagon and thereby ring the bell. The same idea

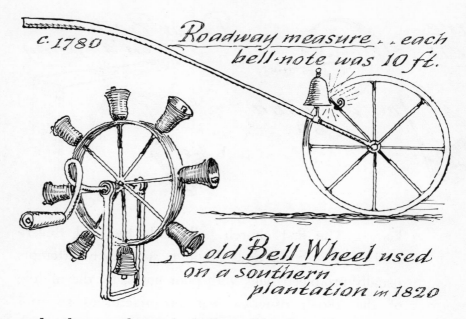

c. 1780

Roadway measure .. each
bell-note was 10 ft.

old Bell Wheel used
on a southern
plantation in 1820

made the storekeeper's bell jingle whenever a customer opened the door and entered. The call bell was for calling the storekeeper when a customer found the store unattended, but it soon became so handy for calling servants to the table, at hotel desks, etc., that one Bevin Brothers catalog of the 1800's listed 108 different types and sizes of call bells.

And so from such tiny bells as call bells and bicycle bells and tea bells to the giants that made the roofs of surrounding buildings shudder when they spoke, bells have had a peculiar place in the lore and history of America. True, all of our earliest bells came from wrecked ships or across the sea, but from the 1800's on, the American bell makers made themselves

Fire Bell on a spring 1760

Door Bell on a spring

known. The first church bell made by Paul Revere was done in 1792 and although such early attempts usually produced bells with poor notes, by the middle of the 1800's America was manufacturing superior bells.

Bell makers in America were different from those of the Old World, for they did their work in a scientific and businesslike manner, whereas many of the European bell makers chose to attach great mystery to their work. Perhaps it was to impress the clergy and whoever bought their bells, or perhaps because they really had rare trade secrets and deserved the prominence their strange habits brought to them.

Some bell casters, such as the famous Bilbie family who made some of the greatest old bells in England, wore their hair halfway down their backs and practiced strange rites or consulted astrology when making or tuning their bells. They put in their bell metal

32

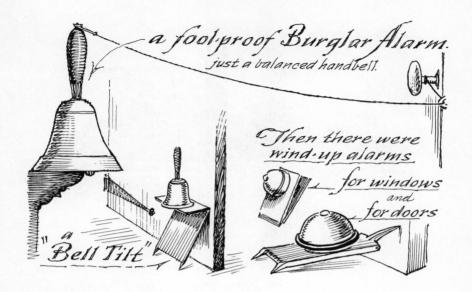

a fool-proof Burglar Alarm.
just a balanced handbell.

Then there were wind-up alarms for windows and for doors

"a Bell Tilt"

such things as dung, hair, gold coins, and "things that can't be spoken of."

When their bells were ordered to match or be in tune with another group of bells, they were known to ask that the existing bells be rung only before dawn, on a certain day when the atmosphere was "just right." Then submerged naked in a nearby pool, with only his head above water, an expert would command the bell to be rung and listen only after the last ripple had smoothed down from the pool's surface. Bells were always hung and first tried out "when the moon was full."

But none of this mumbo-jumbo nonsense was used by the Americans who made bells. They had printed

33

...listening to the bells.

...no such mumbo-jumbo from American bell makers!

catalogs and newspaper advertising just as any other businessmen. By the Civil War era, there came to be a standardized American bell design which many companies manufactured and which came in sizes from "farm size" to "town hall size," schoolhouse and church size. This bell's shoulder was smaller and the lip more flaring than the old European style; many were made simply with mixtures of native irons instead of special bell metal. The drawing shows such a bell along with sizes and prices in the year 1840. Small bells were sold by size, big bells by weight.

With the Civil War many good American customs changed, and among them, the custom of ringing bells on Independence Day. The sounds of guns and

Small shoulder

Flared lip

American Amalgam Bell 1840[c.]

Farm Bells
15 inch diameter .... 5.00.
23 inch 12.00

Church Bells
450 lbs 50.00
850 lbs. 100.00

bombs are much louder than that of bells, and
America had become used to such noise. When the
Civil War ended, firecrackers and aerial bombs had
taken over almost completely and only a very few
of the "old-fashioned people" were left to ring their
bells on the Fourth of July. Some churches carried
on the Independence Day custom, although often
even the people of the town where they rang were
not aware of why the bells were ringing!

Bombs bursting in air

Fireworks have ruled the "Glorious Fourth" for over a century. They began as just bonfires and gunfire, but the Chinese trade brought firecrackers to America in the 1800's. After Civil War days the country was accustomed to the noise of cannonfire and bombs, and the sound of bells on the Fourth of July became an almost completely forgotten custom.

Japan had entered the fireworks scene by then, and "daytime sky displays" became the great Japanese specialty. The idea was to create all sorts of fantastic shapes in the sky, with smoke. A black burst of smoke might make the body of a big spider, while eight blue streaks of smoke radiating outward would indicate legs. Eagles, cuttlefish, snakes, beehives with bees, flags, and all sorts of wonderful shapes could be made with different kinds of explosions and colored smoke.

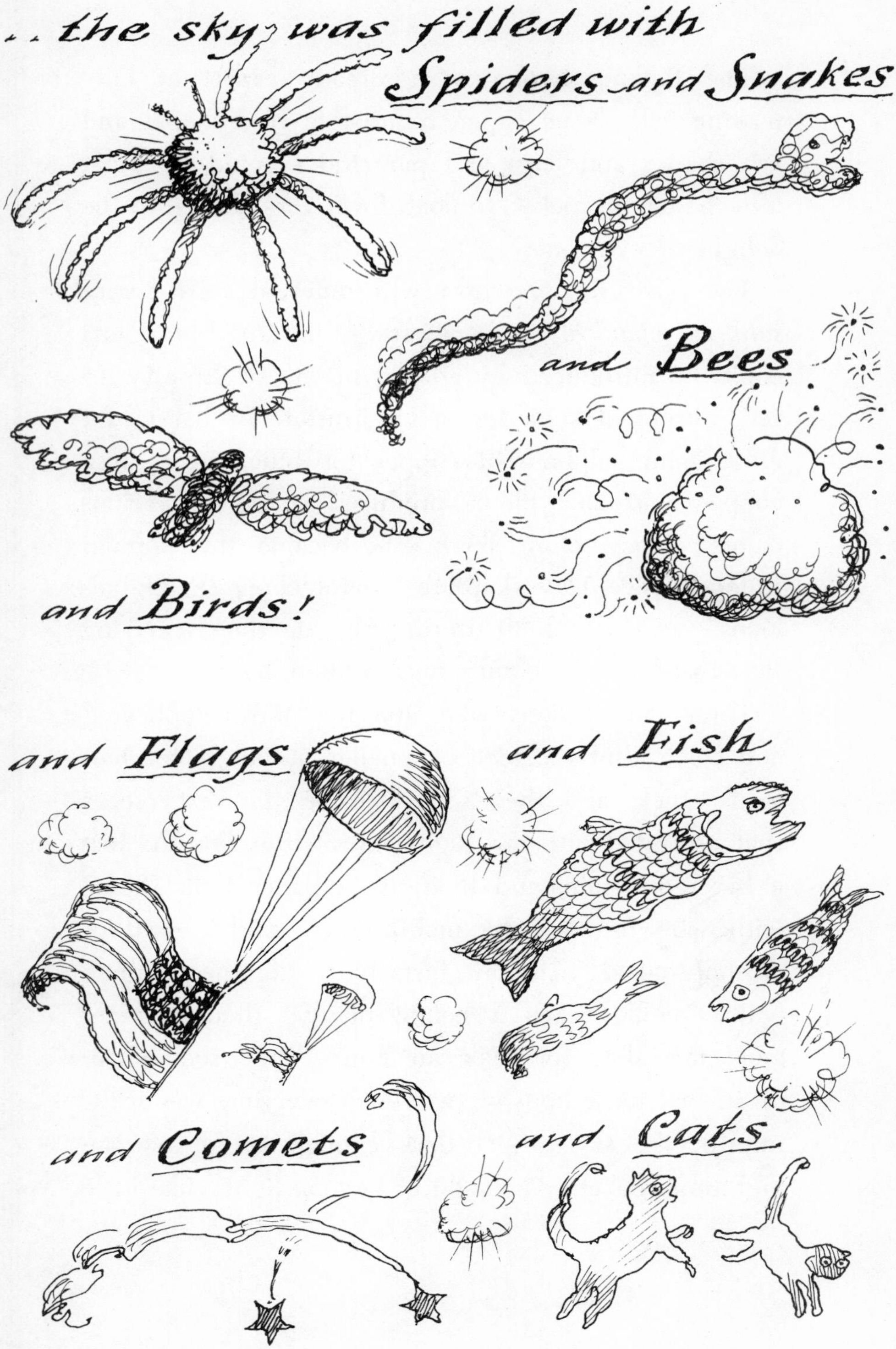

.. the sky was filled with *Spiders* and *Snakes*

and *Bees*

and *Birds!*

and *Flags*

and *Fish*

and *Comets*

and *Cats*

The Japanese, who were already expert at kite-making with tissue paper, found that bird shapes and fish shapes and flags and parachutes could be burst into the air by rocket, to float down very slowly, to the delight of everyone.

The basis for fireworks was different mixtures of *sulphur, charcoal,* and *potassium nitrate,* but colors could be introduced by adding nitrate of strontia for red, nitrate of soda for yellow, nitrate of baryta for green, and sulphate of copper for blue. Steel, iron, copper, and zinc filings produced sparks of various colors. Even before skyrockets became the popular Independence Day skypiece, "pyrotechnic signal balloons" were set aloft during the daytime, carrying slow-fused smoke bombs and colored lights.

These contraptions were too big and complicated and costly, but the idea of smaller hot-air paper balloons stuck, and they soon became the first pieces that ascended into the night sky on the Fourth. Just a big red, white, and blue tissue paper bulb shape, with wire to hold the mouth open, and a wad of alcohol-soaked material furnishing the heat, these ballons could reach a height of two thousand feet and stay aloft for over an hour. They seemed to fill in that tense hour or two when everyone was waiting for the sky to get dark enough to set off the nighttime rockets. The sight of balloon lights, like little

first piece into the night sky...
the *Balloon*

wad of cotton soaked with alcohol.

stars, made the Independence Day sunset a most memorable one.

Balloon time on the Fourth, during the late 1800's and early 1900's, was also the signal for lighting lanterns. People had to see their way around the lawns and verandas. Even if there had been electric lights, they would have shattered the romantic, festive illusion that candles and oil lights brought to any outdoor fete.

What candlelight is to a banquet, colored lamps,

parade torches, and Japanese lanterns were to the old-time Fourth of July night. Copying a Mexican custom, paper bags were sometimes weighted with sand and used as "luminarias" to light walks and driveways or even to outline houses and boathouses. Indeed, in the old days, the night had a special magic and beauty of its own. Singing around a bonfire, picnicking and making the night alive with colored lights seem to be lost arts.

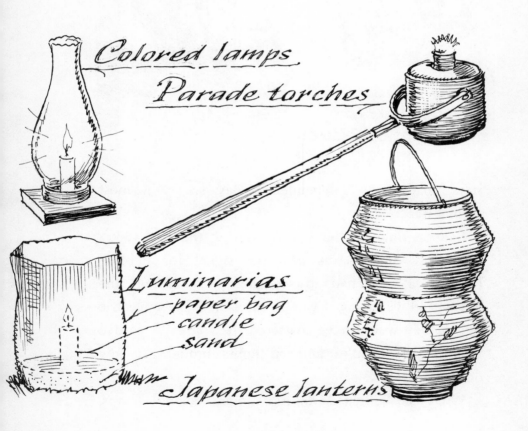

Colored lamps

Parade torches

Luminarias
paper bag
candle
sand

Japanese lanterns

Fireworks, in the old days, were expensive even at a penny a salute, and this was brought home by the quickness of their performance. Even at the height of a rocket's course there was always the twinge of having been a spendthrift, and when the rocket finally burst with a thunderous bang, there was the thought, "Well, there goes another dollar!"

For the smaller children there were sulphur "snakes" which when lit would grow into amazingly

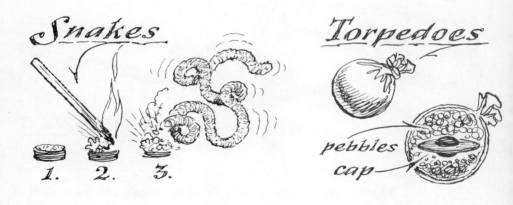

Snakes

1. 2. 3.

Torpedoes

pebbles
cap

long snake-like forms. There were torpedoes that blew up when you threw them down on the sidewalk. During the early 1900's these simple cap-in-pebble devices grew into pretty dangerous "cherry bombs" that were loud enough to wake up a whole neighborhood. It was all dangerous but it was fun.

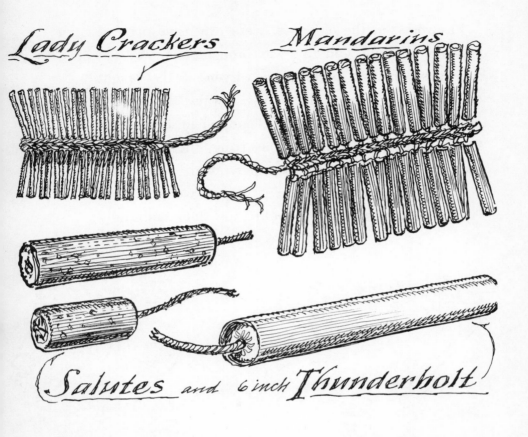

Lady Crackers   *Mandarins*

Salutes and 6 inch Thunderbolt

There were lady crackers that went off like machine-gun fire, bigger "mandarin"-size firecrackers, salutes in thick cardboard, and big six-inch thunderbolts that went off like cannons. Set off under a flat rock, they could turn the rock over; set off under a tin can, they would send the can some thirty feet up. Thrown into water, they would send a spray in every direction for about twenty feet. What could be more exciting?

42

Lifting the can...

You could order your fireworks in sets from a big catalog that a boy could pore through even months before the big event. The names of the night pieces were always fantastic and exciting to the imagination. There were several sizes of "Vesuvius Cascades," "Devil-among-the-tailors," "Whistling Dragons," "Niagara Fountains," "Roman Candles," "Bengal Lights," "Golden Rain," and "Exploding Comets." The boxes they came in were of new white wood that smelled of fresh excelsior and sawdust and the firework pieces would emerge in Chinese gold-flecked paper wrappings.

Just as Christmas has its unwrapping of packages, Independence Day used to have its ceremony of opening packages to lay out on the lawn, ready for proper sequence at the night display. All day long there was the smell of punk, the tang of gunpowder in the air, and the smoldering of cardboard. It was almost as much fun laying out the night pieces as it was setting them off. And when the morning of July fifth arrived, there was always the search for duds, interesting remains, or those that just missed getting fired off. It was a day to be remembered.

Perhaps only mother wanted to forget it, for the Fourth of July was a man's day and except for watching the night display, mother's only participation was

...the sounds of Peace...

to take care of the burns and apply the bandages.

We who remember when Fourth of July fireworks were sold everywhere in the United States miss the fun of shooting them off, but we shall be first to admit that they do make the sound of war, and that bells make a sound of peace and freedom. After all, the sounds of peace are not always loud noises; they are more often like those comforting sounds of America when it was young. Even the Liberty Bell, which is so old and cracked that now it cannot be rung or even struck with a hammer for fear that it might shatter and fall apart, is nevertheless heard in its completely quiet way, in every corner of the civilized world today.

The LIBERTY Bell

that started out as the "Penn Jubilee Bell"

There is a bell that millions of people travel to Philadelphia to see. They touch it with reverence, knowing that they are touching something sacred to the national history. Some stare at it and suddenly burst into tears without really knowing why. Once two blind Japanese soldiers in uniform came "to see" the bell and asked the guide to read the inscription thereon; but the guide led their hands over the raised letters and showed them where the crack was. The guide watched them leave, talking in their own language, and he wondered what they really thought of the bell and its legend. But stuffed carefully in the bell's crack, he found two roses that the veterans had been wearing.

There once was a custom that men remove their hats in the presence of the Liberty Bell, and some still do that. For a bell that does not ring, it is evident that it has become more symbol than bell; perhaps the sound it made in 1776 was strong enough to be heard today by all the peoples of the world.

The bell does not ring because the slightest stroke might shatter the ancient metal into pieces; the last time it was heard, it was struck softly with a rubber mallet. A few years ago, a man in a red fez shouted profanity and struck the bell with a heavy glass paperweight. It nicked the bell metal, and the man was taken away to a mental institution. Recently there was a plot to dynamite the bell.

It is strange that this is perhaps the most well-known bell in the world, yet it is also the one with the least-known history. Very many Americans believe it was made for the occasion of the signing of the Declaration of Independence, or at least that it was made a year or so before the War for Independence.

A controversy is whether it rang at all on July 4, 1776, and the reason for questioning is merely that "there are no records of it having rung on that day." Of course, as the object of that bell was to call people to meeting and to announce the end of each meeting, it was not at all necessary to record every time the bell rang. If the Liberty Bell did not call to meeting on that July 4, and ring the end of that meeting, it would have been unusual indeed. We must presume without doubt that the Liberty Bell rang at least some time on that day. And as the whole town was waiting outside to hear news about the Declaration (and there was no reason for its preparation being secret), those who insist the bell was silent are presuming something very strange. Of course, the Liberty Bell and many other American bells rang when the Declaration was read on the eighth of July, 1776, and all the following July 4— the day finally decided upon to be known as Independence Day.

It is a pity that the history of the great bell has been argued about so much that it has joined the category of doubtful Americana (like the Betsy Ross legend), for its true story is exciting and even more American than most people realize. It started twenty-five years before the Declaration of Independence, and it was ordered to commemorate another declaration called The Charter of Privileges, issued in 1701.

Now in those days when the country was so young, there could not be many hundred-year anniversaries or "centennials"; but there were some fifty-year celebrations that were called jubilees. In fact, the word jubilee once meant a fiftieth-year celebration. The word fifty seemed to have a magic significance to it, and in

Pennsylvania one could vote if he owned fifty acres or had fifty pounds in money; land leases were made out for fifty years, and the fifty acres' dowry was an accepted custom. So when the fiftieth anniversary of the William Penn Charter of Privileges neared in 1751, it seemed a good time for a great jubilee.

This fiftieth-year jubilee was to be in many ways like our present Independence Day, celebrated with bells, gunshots, bonfires by day, and illuminations at night. But the people found some difficulty in choosing a symbol for their jubilee. "Why not make a bell, and inscribe upon it the quotation from Leviticus? Besides, the State House needs a bell."

Nearly everyone was familiar with the Leviticus quotation (25:10) that went, "and ye shall hallow the fiftieth year . . . and it shall be a jubilee unto you." And so it was decided to make a commemorative bell with this quotation upon it.

And then a strange course of events took place. First, it was found that there were no craftsmen in America who made such bells, so the new bell would have to be made in England. But there wasn't enough time, for before the order could reach England and the bell be made and shipped back, the jubilee would be over and forgotten. It was decided that the order go through, but the inscription be changed slightly, taking out that part which mentioned the "fiftieth year" and the reference to "a jubilee."

Isaac Norris, who was Speaker of the Assembly, did the editing, and little did he know that the result would some day refer to another declaration twenty-five years hence. It made the bell not only commemorative of a jubilee but the symbol of a new nation. Here then is the Leviticus quotation (the capital letters spell out what remained after the deletion):

"And ye shall hallow the fiftieth year and PROCLAIM LIBERTY THROUGHOUT ALL THE LAND UNTO ALL THE INHABITANTS THEREOF: it shall be a jubilee unto you and shall return every man unto his possession, and ye shall return every man unto his family."

The bell was cast in early 1752 at the Whitechapel Foundry in England and delivered in the summer of that year, and it was set up in the State House yard for testing. But when it was rung for tone, a crack appeared and the moans of despair were almost as loud as the sound of the bell. The Assembly was going to return it to England, but two workmen offered to melt it and cast it again. "After all," they said, "such a symbol of religious freedom should be made right here in Pennsylvania and not in England. We think we can do a good job."

Actually, they failed to do a good job, for when
John Pass and John Stow tested out their new bell,
it cracked again. But they tried again, adding 1½
ounces of copper for each pound of the old bell's

Respected Friend Robt Charles   Philada. Novr. 1st. 1751

The Assembly having ordered us (the Superintendants of our Statehouse) to procure
a Bell from England to be purchased for their use we take the liberty to apply ourselves
to thee to get us a good Bell of about two thousand pounds weight the cost of
which we presume may amount to abt. One hundred pounds Sterl. or perhaps with the
the Charges something more and accordingly we have now inclosed a first Bell of Exch.a
qr at John Perrin and Son on Messrs Thomas Alcoradens & Compa for £ 100 — Sterling.
we would have chosen to remit a larger Bill at this time, but will take care to
furnish more as soon as we can be informed how much may be wanted

We hope and rely on thy care and assistances in this affair and that there wilt
procure and forward it by the first good oppy. as our Workmen inform us it will be
much less trouble to hang the Bell before their Scaffolds are struck from the Building
where we intend to place it which will not be done'till the end of next Summer or
beginning of the Fall .   Let the Bell be cast by the best Workmen & examined
carefully before it is Shipped with the following words well shaped in large letters
round it vizt
BY order of the Assembly of the Province of Pensylvania for the Statehouse in the City of Philada 1752
                    and underneath.
Proclaim Liberty thro' all the Land to all the Inhabitants thereof Levt XXV · 10 —

As we have experienced thy readiness to serve this province on all occasions We
desire it may be our excuse for this additional trouble from

                              Thy Assured Frds
Let the package for transportation be examined   Isaac Norris
with particular care. and the full value   Signed by an   Thomas Leech
Insured theros   Edward Wooner

metal, and this time the bell was sound. It was the
first time anything like this had been done in America,
and when the bell was hung in State House a great
feast began in the yard below. There is a record
that shows three hundred limes (for punch), three
gallons of rum, a barrel of beer, three pecks of po-
tatoes, forty-four pounds of beef, a fifteen-pound
cheese, and a band of musicians.

The famous bell seemed to ring louder than most
bells. Indeed, there were complaints from nearby
townspeople. In a petition to the Assembly, the bell
was named "a lethal object" and that because of
its "unusual size and sound, it might prove fatal to
those afflicted with sickness." Nevertheless it con-
tinued to call statesmen to meeting and then announce the end of each session. Muffled (as in a
funeral toll) it announced each British tax outrage; it
rang loudly with the news of Lexington and Con-
cord.

On July 4, 1777, the Liberty Bell pealed forth
defiance when the British were preparing an attack

on Philadelphia. On September 14, the Continental Congress realized the danger of invasion and resolved to move all bells from the city, knowing that the British would seek out metal for cannon barrels and ammunition. Where the bells were hidden was kept such a secret that to this day there is doubt about where the Liberty Bell really went. We do know that it left Philadelphia in a caravan of farm wagons, most likely hidden under a load of hay.

Legend has it that the bell was taken to Allentown and hidden beneath the floor of a church. Another story is that the wagon broke under the weight and the bell fell off at Bethlehem, where it was secreted. But there are so many stories about the route taken, that scores of towns in Pennsylvania are known for being the town where the bell was hidden, or through which the bell passed. The truth will never be known. But in the summer of 1778, the bells of Philadelphia were returned, and in 1781 the Liberty Bell, back in its tower, pealed the surrender of Cornwallis at Yorktown.

Some people believe that great bells become humanized with a conscience and that the Liberty Bell always resented the shortening of its Leviticus quotation. Indeed, there have been some strange coincidences connected with the bell's history that might

Ordered in 1751 ...

cast in
London 1752 ...
Philadelphia 1753

bear out such an eerie argument. It managed, for example, to toll the death of all signers of the Declaration of Independence, but when the fiftieth-year jubilee of Independence Day arrived, (July 4, 1826), it tolled the death of both John Adams and Thomas Jefferson. Hardly before one death knell had finished, the toll for the other great man began. It was a startling finish to a jubilee.

In 1835 on July eighth, the anniversary of the bell's biggest day, it tolled the death of John Marshall, the last of the Federalist statesmen who shaped the early Republic. At that moment it cracked.

Postscript

In this day of free verse and abstract art, the painting or writing that tells a complete story is sometimes considered what young people call "square." "Square" and "corny" and "old-fashioned" are words that are often used to belittle things which, when you really think about them, are basic and soul-stirring. The Boy Scouts, the Girl Scouts, the Stars and Stripes, the National Anthem and all the things that keep America alive in the secret corners of our hearts, sometimes bringing a tear of emotion, are frequently considered childish and "square." Of course during war, we display more patriotism; but when times are good, Washington's Birthday is just a sale day at the department stores and Independence Day is a day for fun at the beach and the ball field. Yet at one time such patriotic days had much more meaning. They told a story of America.

The Sound of Bells was written with a purpose, and I hope that the reader will have agreed with me that America's birthday (Independence Day) should be more special and significant than most people regard it. Ringing a bell on July Fourth may seem pretty childish, but it is a beginning. And if the revival of the early American custom of ringing bells on Independence Day will have become established, I would consider this one thing the most important occurrence connected with my life.

In 1963 a resolution passed by the U. S. Congress asks that all bells in the nation, church bells, school bells, town bells, ring together for four minutes at 2 P.M. (E.D.T.) on July Fourth, and governors in their yearly Independence Day proclamations, name the day as a day for the ringing of bells.

If this book adds in any way to the establishment of the custom, I shall be most grateful.

Eric Sloane